EDGE BOOKS™

LABRADOODLES

By Brekka Hervey Larrew

Consultant: Dixie Moore, Owner
Dixie's Doodles, Georgetown, Texas

Capstone press®

Mankato, Minnesota

Edge Books are published by Capstone Press,
151 Good Counsel Drive, P.O. Box 669, Mankato, Minnesota 56002.
www.capstonepress.com

Library of Congress Cataloging-in-Publication Data
Larrew, Brekka Hervey.
    Labradoodles / By Brekka Hervey Larrew.
    p. cm. — (Edge books. All about dogs)
    Includes bibliographical references and index.
    Summary: "Describes the history, physical features, temperament, and
care of the Australian labradoodle breed" — Provided by publisher.
    ISBN-13: 978-1-4296-2009-3 (hardcover)
    ISBN-10: 1-4296-2009-9 (hardcover)
    1. Labradoodle — Juvenile literature. I. Title. II. Series.
SF429.L29L37 2009
636.72 — dc22   2008005273

Editorial Credits
Jenny Marks, editor; Veronica Bianchini, designer; Marcie Spence,
    photo researcher

Photo Credits
AP Images/Mary Godleski, 26; *The Plain Dealer*, Joshua Gunter, 24
Capstone Press/Karon Dubke, cover, 1, 5 (poodle and Labrador
    retriever), 16, 22, 23, 29
Courtesy of Wally Conron, 9
Getty Images Inc./LWA, 19, 21
iStockphoto/Alister Beveridge, 15
Ron Kimball Stock/Lynn M. Stone, 25
Shutterstock/Jeanne Hatch, 6–7; Susan Harris, 18
Tegan Australian Labradoodles, 5 (Labradoodle), 10, 11, 12, 13, 14,
17,
    20, 28

Capstone Press gives special thanks to Martha Diedrich, dog trainer.

1 2 3 4 5 6 13 12 11 10 09 08

Table of Contents

CHAPTER 1

A DESIGNER DOG

Fashion designers aren't the only people setting trends these days. Dog breeders have created designer dogs too. A designer dog is a **crossbreed** of two or more purebred dogs. Designer dogs are popular, and the Labradoodle is one of the hottest of them all.

By crossing Labrador retrievers with poodles, the resulting dogs have excellent **traits**. Families love Labradoodles for their loyalty and friendliness. Since many of the dogs don't shed, owners enjoy cleaner floors and furniture. Labradoodles are smart and easily trained. They make great guide dogs for the blind. Also, some people are allergic to the skin and hair that dogs shed. These people can often live with a low-shedding dog like a Labradoodle.

crossbreed — a planned mix of two or more breeds
trait — a quality or characteristic

Labradoodles have a mix of the best qualities of poodles and Labrador retrievers.

EDGE FACT

Some celebrities can be counted among the Labradoodle's fans. Jennifer Aniston, Tiger Woods, and Christie Brinkley all own Labradoodles.

Labradoodle puppies look a little like both of their parents.

Despite their popularity, not everyone thinks that breeding Labradoodles is a good idea. Some purebred dog lovers consider Labradoodles to be expensive mutts that don't meet purebred standards. Kennel clubs like the American Kennel Club (AKC) refuse to register Labradoodles as purebred dogs. They claim the puppies don't have consistent enough traits. Breeders are working hard to fine-tune Labradoodles so they can predict the puppies' size, coat type, and color. Labradoodle fans and breeders alike hope that one day their favorite dogs will be accepted as their own breed.

CHAPTER 2

THE LABRADOODLE'S BEGINNINGS

In the early 1980s, Pat Blum searched for the right **guide dog**. Pat was blind and needed a dog to help her get around. But her husband suffered from severe dog allergies. She needed a guide dog that wouldn't make her husband sick. Though she lived in Hawaii, she wrote a letter to the Royal Guide Dog Association of Australia. She asked if they could produce an **allergy**-free guide dog for her.

Wally Conron, a breeding expert who worked for the association, thought it would be an easy assignment. He knew that poodles were non-shedding, trainable work dogs. Many people with allergies can live with poodles. He sent 33 hair and saliva samples from different poodles to Blum. Surprisingly, her husband was allergic to all of them.

allergy — sensitivity to something in the environment that causes itchy eyes, a runny nose, and other symptoms

guide dog — a dog that has been trained to assist and guide people with special needs

Breeder Wally Conron plays with one of his first Labradoodles.

Finally, after two years, Conron crossbred a standard poodle with a white Swedish Labrador retriever. In 1989, three puppies were born. One of these proved non-allergic for the woman's husband. This puppy, Sultan, was then trained as a guide dog. He was a perfect fit for both Blum and her husband.

A Tough Sell

Meanwhile, Conron had difficulty placing the other two puppies in foster homes. Puppies who will become guide dogs must spend 12 to 18 months in foster homes before they begin training. They learn how to behave and get along with people. Conron had a list of people who wanted to foster a purebred dog. However, finding a home for crossbred puppies proved to be a tough sell.

Conron came up with a clever idea. He decided to name the dogs Labradoodles. Then he went on TV to try to find foster homes for the remaining puppies. He advertised the dogs as allergy-free guide dogs. Suddenly, many people began lining up to get a Labradoodle.

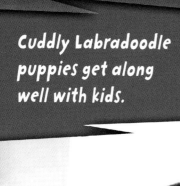

Cuddly Labradoodle puppies get along well with kids.

EDGE FACT

Pat Blum looked for a guide dog from Australia because rabies is not found in Australia or Hawaii. In Hawaii, animals from Australia are considered to be safe from rabies. They can go right home with their owners.

A Developing Breed

Breeders across Australia tried to fill the public's new demand for Labradoodles. Many bred Labrador retrievers with poodles regardless of the dogs' health and personalities. A large number of the puppies were born with the shedding coat of a Labrador retriever. Many also developed health problems such as **hip dysplasia** and eye diseases.

Labradoodles are loyal and easy to train.

hip dysplasia — a painful and crippling condition of a dog's hip joint

Two Labradoodle breeding and research Manor and Tegan Park, opened in Australi breeders worked hard to raise excellent do of their puppies shed. Some caused proble sufferers. Only the best puppies were used for breeding.

Over the years, other breeds were mixed with Australian Labradoodles. These included American and English cocker spaniels, Irish water spaniels, and curly-coated retrievers. The breeding helped strengthen desirable traits like a stocky build and a thinner coat. It also produced Labradoodles with new colors, like dark chocolate.

Today, Labradoodle breeders encourage good breeding practices. They watch the health of the dogs and keep records of their dogs' ancestry. They try to breed dogs that have a standard appearance and personality. After many generations of breeding, Labradoodle puppies rarely shed. Health problems have become less common, too.

CHAPTER 3

WHAT is A LABRADOODLE?

Striving for a Standard

There are several reasons why the AKC doesn't yet accept Labradoodles as a breed. One is that the puppies don't have consistent traits. Breeders are fine-tuning Labradoodles so that they can fix this problem. Also, the AKC requires that 300 dogs from 20 states be registered. These dogs must be multigenerational. This means they must have parents and grandparents who are Labradoodles. According to the AKC, a national breed club must also support breeders and dog owners. In time the number of Labradoodles and owners will grow, and the AKC conditions will be met.

After many generations of breeding, Labradoodle traits have become much more consistent than in the past. A Labradoodle's head resembles that of a Labrador retriever, but it is less blocky. A Labradoodle's ears hang flat against its head. Its large, expressive eyes seek eye contact with people. Its big, square nose is usually rose-colored or black.

Labradoodles have big, square noses.

Labradoodles are known for their soft, wavy coats.

Labradoodles were originally bred for an allergy-friendly coat, so their fur is their most important trait. Labradoodles have three types of coats. The most desirable is the fleece coat. This non-shedding coat forms loose spirals. It is extremely soft and silky. Also desirable is the wool-curly coat. This non-shedding coat is similar to a poodle's coat. It requires more grooming than the fleece coat. The least desirable type of coat is the hair coat. Like a Labrador retriever's coat, hair coats shed year-round.

Labradoodles' coats can be many colors. Some dogs have black, cream, red, gold, silver, or chocolate fur. Others are pale chalk, tan café au lait, cool blue, or rosy apricot. Most Labradoodles are one solid color, but some are **parti-color**.

parti-color — having one main color with patches of one or more other colors

There are three sizes of Labradoodles. The first is the standard Labradoodle, a Labrador retriever crossbred with a standard poodle. These dogs stand 21 to 24 inches (53 to 61 centimeters) at the shoulders and weigh from 50 to 65 pounds (23 to 30 kilograms). In 1998, Tegan Park used a miniature poodle to help create miniature Labradoodles. These dogs are less than 16 inches (41 centimeters) tall and weigh less than 25 pounds (11 kilograms). Finally, medium labradoodles were created by crossing a standard Labradoodle with a miniature labradoodle. Medium dogs are about 17 to 20 inches (43 to 51 centimeters) tall and weigh 30 to 45 pounds (14 to 20 kilograms).

Labradoodles come in many colors, coats, and sizes.

Temperament

Labradoodles are smart and easily trained. They enjoy work and are loyal to their families. Being work dogs, they are active and need exercise. Many toys interest them, especially chew toys with a treat hidden inside. Labradoodles are quick to learn tricks. Some fun tricks include chasing their tail, shaking hands, and waving their paws on command. Labradoodles also enjoy learning games. During games, dogs exercise their brains and their bodies. Fetch and frisbee are fun, easy games people can play with their Labradoodles.

Playing fetch is a fun, active way to bond with Labradoodles.

Labradoodles often seem to recognize how their owners are feeling. When an owner is sad, a Labradoodle may give kisses. When owners are angry, they may hide. These dogs strive to please, so punishing a Labradoodle can easily hurt its feelings. Using positive training methods works best.

Labradoodles are friendly, social animals. They don't enjoy being alone. They prefer being with people and other animals. A good romp at a dog park usually makes them happy. They also enjoy simply sitting at their owner's feet or on their owner's lap.

Labradoodles enjoy spending time with their owners.

CHAPTER 4

CARING FOR A LABRADOODLE

A pet's health is very important. Labradoodles should see a veterinarian every year to be **vaccinated**. Veterinarians also care for Labradoodles when they get sick. Hip dysplasia is the biggest health problem for Labradoodles. Other health problems may include heart disease, eye disease, and ear infections. Some dogs also develop elbow or knee problems. Many dog owners choose to have a veterinarian **spay** or **neuter** their pets. This prevents their pets from having unwanted puppies. It also helps pets live longer by reducing their risk of cancer.

vaccinate — to give an injection that protects against disease

spay/neuter — an operation to prevent an animal from having young; males are neutered and females are spayed.

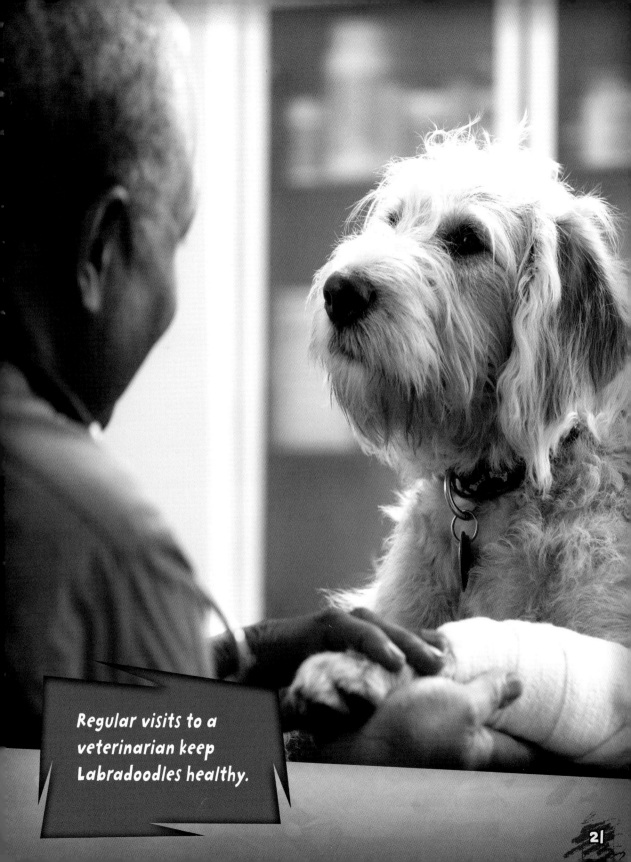

Regular visits to a veterinarian keep Labradoodles healthy.

High-quality food can help keep your Labradoodle healthy for years to come.

Feeding

To stay healthy, Labradoodles need a high-quality diet. Owners should select a dog food with meat listed in the first three ingredients. These ingredients could include lamb, chicken, beef, or even fish. Foods containing corn, wheat, and hulls should be avoided. They often trigger allergies that make dogs itchy and sick.

Young puppies should eat three meals a day. Once they are 5 to 6 months old, two meals a day are enough. To keep a dog on a healthy eating schedule, many people remove uneaten food after 15 to 30 minutes. However, fresh water should be available at all times.

Grooming

The amount of grooming a Labradoodle needs depends upon its coat type. Fleece and wool coats require weekly brushing and should be trimmed two to three times per year. Hair coats need monthly brushing but no trimming.

Labradoodles need baths only two to three times per year. Too much bathing strips healthy oils from the dog's coat. The oils repel water and keep the dog's skin soft.

Exercise

Exercise keeps Labradoodles fit and healthy. Leash walks are an important part of their daily routine. Plus, Labradoodles enjoy the variety of sights, sounds, and smells they discover on walks. Frequent leash-free exercise satisfies the dogs' need for activity. Hiking, biking, or taking a trip to a dog park provide fun, leash-free exercise.

Labradoodles can also compete in agility and flyball contests. In agility competitions, dogs race through courses featuring seesaws, tunnels, jumps, and other obstacles. Flyball is a sport that began in the late 1960s. Teams of dogs retrieve a ball and return it to their owners in a relay race.

Labradoodles need plenty of exercise.

Labradoodles learn very quickly and make excellent guide dogs.

Training

Labradoodles are fast learners. It takes only a few repetitions to teach Labradoodles basic commands like "sit," "stay," "come," and "**heel**." While in training, the dog should receive a reward for each success. Rewards can include treats, toys, affection, and verbal praise. Earning rewards makes the dog want to repeat the behavior.

To ensure training success, lessons should be kept short and fun. **Obedience** classes can help owners learn to use appropriate training techniques. Outside of obedience class, rules must be followed closely by all members of a Labradoodle's family. Family members should work together to help their dog learn the best way to behave.

Well-trained Labradoodles can compete in obedience trials. In these contests, dogs must heel, stay, come, and obey other commands. More advanced contests require dogs to perform jumps and sniff out specific scents.

heel — to follow behind on command
obedience — ability and willingness
to do what is asked

Labradoodles make excellent work dogs. They are popular guide dogs for the blind. They often work as assistance dogs to retrieve items for people in wheelchairs. They also work as therapy dogs, bringing cheer to the elderly and sick. And of course, they make great pets for active families.

Labradoodles are growing more and more popular. Labradoodle clubs have registered breeders in many countries. Breeders are working hard to gain AKC acceptance of Labradoodles as a breed. With time, the AKC and other kennel clubs may recognize these lovable designer dogs as an official breed. If not, Labradoodle lovers everywhere will still know that this one-of-a-kind dog is a perfect pet.

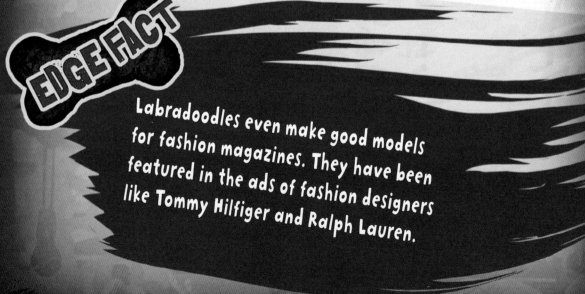

EDGE FACT

Labradoodles even make good models for fashion magazines. They have been featured in the ads of fashion designers like Tommy Hilfiger and Ralph Lauren.

Labradoodles are fun, loyal pets for active families.

Glossary

agility (uh-JIL-uh-tee) — the ability to move quickly and easily

allergy (AL-ur-jee) — sensitivity to something in the environment that causes itchy eyes, a runny nose, and other symptoms

consistent (kuhn-SISS-tuhnt) — uniform; the same for all members of the group.

crossbreed (KROSS-breed) — a planned mix of two or more breeds

guide dog (GIDE DOG) — a dog that has been trained to assist and guide people with special needs

heel (HEEL) — to follow behind on command

hip dysplasia (HIP dis-PLAY-see-uh) — a painful and crippling condition of a dog's hip joint

multigenerational (mul-ti-gen-ur-RAY-shun-uhl) — describes a dog whose ancestors are the same breed as itself

mutt (MUT) — a dog born from a random mixture of breeds

neuter (NOO-tur) — an operation to prevent an animal from having young

obedience (oh-BEE-dee-uhnss) — the willingness and ability to do what is asked

parti-color (PAR-tee-KUHL-ur) — having one main color with patches of one or more other colors

spay (SPAY) — an operation to prevent a female animal from having young

trait (TRAYT) — a quality or characteristic

vaccinate (VAK-suh-nate) — to give an injection that protects against disease

Read More

Bennett Woolf, Norma. *Hot Dogs!: Fourteen of the Top Designer Dogs.* Hauppauge, N.Y.: Barrons, 2007.

MacAulay, Kelley, and Bobbie Kalman. *Labrador Retrievers.* Pet Care. New York: Crabtree, 2007.

Wheeler, Jill C. *Labradoodles.* Dogs. Edina, Minn.: Abdo, 2008.

Internet Sites

FactHound offers a safe, fun way to find Internet sites related to this book. All of the sites on FactHound have been researched by our staff.

Here's how:

1. Visit *www.facthound.com*
2. Choose your grade level.
3. Type in this book ID **1429620099** for age-appropriate sites. You may also browse subjects by clicking on letters, or by clicking on pictures and words.
4. Click on the **Fetch It** button.

FactHound will fetch the best sites for you!

Index

allergies, 4, 8, 10, 13, 16, 22
American Kennel Club
  (AKC), 7, 14, 28
appearance, 13, 15, 16

Blum, Pat, 8, 9, 11
breeders, 7, 8, 12, 13, 14, 28

coats, 7, 12, 16, 23
    fleece, 13, 16
    hair, 16
    parti-color, 16
    wool-curly, 16
competitions, 24, 27
Conron, Wally, 8–10
crossbreeding, 4

designer dogs, 4, 7, 28

exercise, 18, 24, 25

food, 22
foster homes, 10

grooming, 23
guide dogs, 4, 8, 9, 10, 26, 28

health problems, 12, 13, 20
hip dysplasia, 12

obedience classes, 27

neutering, 20

personality. *See* temperament,
puppies, 7, 9, 10, 12, 13, 14,
    20, 22.

rabies, 11
Royal Guide Dog Association, 8
Rutland Manor, 13

shedding, 4, 12, 13, 16
size, 7, 17
spaying, 20
Sultan, 9

Tegan Park, 13, 17
temperament, 4, 12, 13, 18–19
toys, 18
training, 4, 9, 10, 18, 19, 27

vaccinations, 20
veterinary care, 20, 21

ML   3/09